THAT'S MY COLOR

Discover Your 5 Signature Colors and Transform Your Life

Jen Thoden

D1526961

Jen Thoden
Best Selling Author, Speaker, Entrepreneur

**That's My Color Discover Your 5 Signature Colors
and Transform Your Life**

by Jen Thoden
Copyright © 2018 by Jennifer Thoden

ISBN: 9781717844736

For more information about Your Color Style,
please visit:
https://YourColorStyle.com

Table of Contents

Dear Reader

"Follow your passion. Stay true to yourself. Never follow someone else's path unless you're in the woods and you're lost and you see a path. By all means, you should follow that."

Ellen DeGeneres

This is NOT a book about color!

Wait, what?

OK, OK, there's color in this book, and I'm going to say a lot about color. But this is really a book about discovery and transformation.

The more conversations I have with my color clients—women in their mid-forties and fifties—the more I realize that the desire for more color in their wardrobe is actually an expression of their craving for a more color-filled life.

I have a great life now, but it wasn't always this way. A few years ago, I went from having three kids to two, married to divorced, big house to small, and from self-employed to a cubicle.

This book is the story of how I used color to rediscover myself and create the life I wanted.

But this book isn't just about me. It's about YOU. It's about your power to rediscover yourself and reinvent your life with color. In fact, you can do this with just five colors. Read on to uncover each of them and learn how to infuse it into your world.

Want to see how this works?

Imagine for a moment that you wake up in a bad mood. Maybe you had a stressful dream or there's that nagging worry about something. You look in the mirror and you don't like what you see. Maybe your tummy is bulging. You have cellulite. Your breasts are sagging. You look tired and old. Your mood has you seeing a negative image of yourself. As your day continues, you begin to see things that support this mood. Your kid is wearing the same t-shirt and shorts for the fourth day in a row and hasn't taken a shower in who knows how long. The barista gets your coffee order wrong (ok, this is a first-world problem but still…). Traffic is crazy on the way to work and you're almost out of gas. Negative emotions radiate from you and you will continue to find negative events throughout the day.

Now, let's try that again.

Imagine that you wake up in that same bad mood. You go through that same checklist of everything wrong with how you look. But this time you force yourself to put on a blouse in a color that you've been told looks good on you. Maybe a fun pair of shoes. Looking in the mirror, you see yourself a bit differently. Your mood shifts a bit. You might even get a compliment at work. This time, your confidence builds and you actually find good things happening to you throughout the day.

Same wakeup mood, but which outcome do you prefer?

The thing is, who you are right now and how you see yourself is based on everything that's happened in your life up to this point. But you can change it!

What if you could transform your life just by taking some small steps?

If there's one thing I want you to take away after reading this book, it is this: You have the ability to create the life that you'll love. It might not be clear to you yet, but trust me on this!

That's My Color!

It can all start with one simple color choice.

The Coaching Call

❊ ❊ ❊

I sat in the middle of an unmade bed with my laptop in front of me, staring at my phone with dread. I was so nervous! I'd signed up for a life coaching program because I had been unhappy for a long time and I wanted to live a better life. But in that moment, I had no idea what to expect.

Taking a deep breath, I dialed the number.

Nervously tapping my fingers on the edge of my laptop, I waited for a couple of minutes until a man's voice welcomed the group to the call. He introduced himself and asked each of us to say our name and answer the question: "Who are you?"

Who are we? Who am I? Umm, what should I say? I have no idea!

Panic gripped my chest and I typed my name into the laptop just in case I forgot it when it was my turn to talk. Hey, it can happen!

I listened to each person say their name and something like, "I'm a mother, painter, business owner, and lover of life."

Thank you, lover of life! Now what am I supposed to say? Lover of whole pints of ice cream that I eat while binge-watching The Bachelor? *Hater of chicken wings because I don't like to work that hard when I eat?*

There were six people on the call including myself, and I was sure that I was the only one not prepared with an answer. I almost hung up. It would be so easy! "Oh, I'm sorry, wrong number!"

When it was my turn to speak, I loudly stated my name with a nervous giggle, "Hi! I'm Jennifer Thoden!" I thought my loudness might hide my lack of confidence.

I began to ramble on about having two kids, being divorced, having just moved into a new house, on and on...

Should I tell them I once had three kids but lost one to cancer? Is that too much information? Is that what defines me? No. I'd better not say that.

"Pause," I heard the coach say.

Pause? Oh no! What did I just say? How long have I been talking?

"So who ARE you?" he asked patiently.

I sat in silence as blood rushed to my face. Embarrassed, I whispered, "I don't know," and braced myself to be scolded.

Instead, the coach responded gently, "That's perfect. That's why we're here. Today we're going to talk about our values and who we really are. What makes us tick? What's important to us?"

I felt like such an idiot.

How could I not know who I really am and what's important to me? Who was I anyway?

As a child, I wanted to be an artist. A cartoonist, actually. I used to watch cartoons on TV with sheets of white paper and markers in front of me. I learned to draw the cartoons I'd see on the screen. I'd do this for hours, until my mother decided it was better to be playing outside than watching TV for hours. Ok fine.

As I got older, I had grand visions of being an animator for Disney or Pixar.

I went to Art School. Majored in animation. Got married. Moved to San Francisco. Got a job at a gaming company as a character animator. Do you remember Petz? No? Well, I worked on that game! Anyway, I was on my way. Pixar, here I come!

Not so fast.

I did not become a famous character artist for Pixar, because life happened to me.

I got pregnant. My husband and I moved back to Virginia. We had three children in four years. He traveled a lot for work. My life consisted of diapers, pull-ups, snack time, nap time, timeouts, laundry, fist-pounding tantrums, and tears. Those last two were not exclusive to my children.

I was exhausted. I'm sure there were a lot of happy moments, but I was moving at full speed just to keep up. In addition to mommy duty, I had to get up every morning, pull myself together, and go to work.

I mastered pushing a double stroller, holding my oldest child by the hand, grocery shopping, feeding the baby her bottle, and picking up spilled Cheerios all at the same time. "How do you do it?" people would ask with wonder.

I earned the title of Supermom very early and I wore it like a badge of honor. I liked being seen as this strong, she-can-do-anything woman.

When my children were 7, 4, and 2 we moved to Ft. Worth, Texas. Then life happened to me again. Within the first week of moving there, my oldest child, Kelley, was diagnosed with osteosarcoma.

Cancer.

To deal with the fear of losing my daughter to cancer, I chose *not* to deal with it. Instead, I spent the next two years and three months being Supermom. I spent endless nights in the hospital with Kelley. I took her to all of her doctor's appointments. I administered all of the home medications. When I was home, I felt guilty for not being there for my other two children. So I cooked. I cleaned. Did I mention that I'd started an online business right before we moved to Texas? So I worked on that in my spare time, too. Ha! Spare time!

People would marvel at me.

"How do you do it?"
"You are so strong!"
"No way I could do all that!"

The Supermom image was like a drug I needed to keep going.

Kelley lost her fight with cancer at the age of nine, and I dealt with this loss by filling the void with even more noise. We moved back to Virginia where I made it my mission to make sure everyone was happy.

Everyone but me, that is.

I didn't want to face the fact that my marriage was suffering, so I focused on being the perfect mom, homemaker, and business owner. Still, it was clear my husband wasn't happy either. Thinking that more stability would make things better, I sold my business and went back to work full-time. It didn't get better.

We separated right after Christmas in 2012.

I was running on autopilot, staying busy. Making sure the kids were okay. Making sure my parents were okay. Making sure my friends still wanted to be my friends. I even worried about my ex-husband, since I was the one that left. More guilt.

It was go-go-go, until the kids spent the first few days of the new year with their dad, and all of a sudden...

There was nothing.

I was alone in my townhouse. No kids. Nobody to tell me how strong and amazing I was. Just me.

How did I get here?

The walls seemed to close in as a series of terrible memories began to play in my mind. The phone call telling me that Kelley had cancer. All those doctor's appointments. Choking back tears when the nurse told me they were fighting for my little girl's life. Seeing my little angel just moments after she took her last breath. Trying to make everybody happy.

Then, I remembered those long tearful nights as we struggled to keep our marriage together. And I remembered the moment I chose to leave.

Now what? Seriously, what in the world am I going to do now?

I was divorced with two kids. I'd put on weight. I looked and felt awful. I was empty and lost. My life seemed completely drained of color.

I felt sad, lonely, angry, guilty, frustrated, and just unhappy.

Who am I when I'm not Supermom?

I came to a sharp realization that I was not living an authentic life. How could I, when I had completely ignored myself for more than sixteen years? The life I had been living was for everyone else, and very little of it was for me. When you discover that the person you've been showing to the world is not the person you truly are or the person you want to be, it can really set you off-balance.

A recent study conducted by the Centers for Disease Control and Prevention found that women between the ages 40 and 59 have the highest rate of depression out of any age group or gender in the United States. In fact, middle-aged people are the least happy, have the lowest levels of life satisfaction, and report the highest levels of anxiety.

So it's no mystery why we see people going through an identity crisis in their middle age, aka the midlife crisis. But have you actually considered why this happens?

Imagine having four layers. Like Russian nesting dolls. Four dolls, each one inside another.

Our outer layer is the costume we wear every day. This is who we present to the world. It could be Supermom, like I tried to be. Or maybe it's the successful business owner. Or the perfect loving wife. Or maybe the jokester. A storyteller. The cheerleader.

This is our persona. It's how people would describe us.

For my highly-scientific look at this, see Figure 1.0.

Figure 1.0 - My Costume

Our second layer is who we are when we're alone and we take the costume off. We are a sea of emotions that the costume does a magical job of hiding. For me, I was feeling sad, tired, guilty, lonely, frustrated, angry, scared, and unloved.

Emotions are temporary, unless they become a habit. It's especially easy to develop a habit of feeling certain negative emotions on a consistent basis. For example, you might often feel angry or victimized.

These are emotions we are feeling for sure, but they do not define us. We may feel angry, but we are not anger. We may feel victimized, but we are not victims. Nor are we guilt, loneliness, or frustration.

Want to see what I look like without my costume? I bet you do! See Figure 1.1.

That's My Color!

Figure 1.1 - No costume

Your third layer is your ego, that stubborn controlling bitch under your emotions. More on her in a moment.

Figure 1.2 - My bitchy controlling ego

Your innermost layer—the core—is you. This is your true authentic self. This is who you have been all your life. For me, this is my inner artist. My creative spirit. The giggler. Lover of games and fun.

Figure 1.3 - Me!

What happens to many of us is that we get so focused on the costume we wear for everyone else that we stop focusing on ourselves. We forget about our core. We don't have time for her. And we crush her spirit beneath three layers of, well, I think the technical term is 'crap.'

It only takes a moment for you to wake up and realize that your costume doesn't match your core. There's a huge gap.

That moment typically follows an event that snaps us out of autopilot and forces the realization that we don't like the emotions we've been feeling. We don't like who we've become. We don't know who we are anymore. We start asking questions like, "What is all of this for? Who am I? What makes me happy?"

You have a choice when you feel this imbalance. You can choose to get to know yourself again and close the gap. Or you can put even more energy into keeping up your costume. Maybe you get a fancy car or motorcycle. Go on a shopping spree. Having an affair. This is the classic midlife crisis, because it often happens in middle age. We try so hard to hold on to the costume we have spent a lifetime wearing, but it's exhausting.

So, as I sat alone in my quiet home, realizing that I'd lost myself somewhere along the road of life, I made the choice to get to know myself again. To get back to my true self, back to whatever brings me joy.

I'd like to share with you my journey to find myself again, and how I closed that gigantic gap between my true self and the Supermom costume I wore.

Oh wait! Before we dive in, I need to tell you about your bitchy, controlling ego—that third layer I mentioned a moment ago. Here's what's going to happen: As you begin to do things that you truly enjoy doing and as you become more aware of your true self, and maybe even while you're reading this book, your emotional layer is going to change too. Emotions of anger may be replaced with emotions of happiness.

When this change starts to happen, it's likely that your bitchy, controlling ego is going to panic because she doesn't like change. She likes things to stay exactly the way they are right now. It's all she knows. She has no reason to change it. It's all about her, not about you.

Figure 1.4 - It's all about her

As soon as she senses change, she will jump in and try to change it back. She's the voice in your head that says things like:

"It's okay. You don't need to do that now. Do it later."

"That's silly. How is drawing or painting going to bring you joy? That's for kids."

"You're not strong enough to do that on your own. You don't do well alone."

"It's okay if you have this one cookie. It's just this one time."

"You're tired. You can go running tomorrow. Just watch TV instead."

Figure 1.5 - Just eat the cookie!

Sound familiar?

I recommend you make it a goal to be aware of her and to remember that she is not in charge. You are. You are

25

the commander of your ship. The queen of your kingdom. The designer of your life.

So, how do you get to know yourself again? And how do you get your ego out of the way? Where do you start?

You start with small accomplishments. With each personal success you get to know yourself a little more. You feed power back into yourself. You build your self confidence. Your emotions shift and change. You begin to replace your emotions with feelings of empowerment, confidence, happiness, excitement and joy.

Color and creativity are woven throughout my personal journey of self discovery. I didn't realize it as I went through these experiences, but looking back I see how color played a huge part in my transformation.

Each signature color that I share with you will have a profound effect on all four layers of you. As you learn about the signature colors, you will get to decide which colors truly resonate with you and which ones hold emotional triggers for you with positive or negative memories.

Each time you make a personal choice, you get to know yourself a little bit more. These authentic colors will change how people react to you in a positive way. This positive change will have you feeling better, which will boost your self-confidence.

You will begin to transform into the person you want to be—or maybe you will just bring that amazing core of colors to the surface and let it transform the rest of your life.

See ya, sad, angry, discouraged, frustrated, unhappy self!

Jen Thoden

Your Eye-Poppin' Colors

❖ ❖ ❖

I walked downstairs to make myself a cup of coffee on a beautiful Saturday fall morning. Steamy brew in hand, I looked around to find a spot to enjoy it and then remembered that the only furniture I had was in the living room.

Ugh. That room is so boring!

I'd been living in my own townhouse for three months and that living room *wasn't* a room I wanted to be in. I stood there sipping my coffee and looking around, noticing how the energy I was getting from the delicious coffee and peppermint-mocha creamer was being drained away by the overwhelming blandness of the space I was in.

Did I make decaf by mistake?

It's not that the room didn't have potential. There were three pretty arched windows, a crown moulding, and chair rail. But it also had builder-white walls and a beige sectional. No energy. No spirit. Completely flat!

No color! That's what's wrong here!

"I'm going to paint these walls," I declared to absolutely no one. Creativity has always been one of my core values.

This is my place and I can do anything I want with it!

Just the thought of adding color to the room got me fired up!

Oh yes, this is happening today! Right the heck now!

Actually, I might have used a different word there…

But what color?

All of a sudden, panic exploded in my chest.

Why is this so scary? I knew immediately. *It's because I lived with him for so long.*

For years, I'd been married to a man who was against doing anything to the walls in our home. No paint, no pictures, no holes in the walls. We would have arguments over it. I'd want to paint the walls a harmless cream color and he'd declare it yellow. He only wanted white. I wanted a house with accent walls of color and bright-colored prints; but any time I'd propose a color or get ready to hang a picture, we'd have those same stupid arguments.

White walls. No paint, no pictures, no holes in the walls. After a while, I stopped trying.

Well, he's not here now! No more white walls!

I pulled out the color swatches I'd been collecting for a while and sifted through them. A light teal color seemed to draw me to it and I imagined that color on my living room walls.

Yes! This is it!

Umm, it sure is a lot of color though…

But it was just paint. What was the worst that could happen? I'd paint that color and hate it?

After a quick visit to the store for paint, brushes, tape, rollers, and drop cloths, I had everything I needed to turn the room into an expression of myself. I popped the top off of one of the cans of paint.

Ahhhhh… I love this color!

It was a little bluer and softer than I'd originally imagined but it was so pretty!

I loaded up a roller with paint and slowly stepped towards the builder-white wall, almost expecting the wall to retreat like a scared dog.

Here we go!

I watched fresh, rich teal roll onto dull white.

Oh crap! This is way darker than I expected!

Luckily I kept going. I wanted to get one wall done and then decide if it was the wrong color. I put some country music on—Rascal Flatts is great painting music!—and sang along out loud and off-key, "Life is a highway!"

The more color the wall took on, the more I loved it.

See ya, builder white! Hello, color!

I didn't stop until the first coat was done. I walked out of the room to clear my head, suddenly noticing that my arms were sore. My hands were cramped up. I was exhausted. After eating a turkey sandwich to recharge, I popped open a cold beer, walked back into the living room, and froze. I almost dropped the beer.

Is this really my living room?

It was breathtaking! The arched windows were defined. The mouldings popped. The room seemed to wrap itself around me with energy and personality.

It's perfect.

It had seemed too dark at first because there was no energy in those dull white walls. But now there was balance in the room. *My* room.

I started on the second coat and another memory came back.

When we lived in Texas, I was itching to do something creative. I didn't want a fight, but I had to do something to break up those boring white walls. Deciding on a mural, I found some paper and sketched out a lovely Tuscany-inspired stone window that looked out to a vineyard on rolling hills. I copied the drawing to the wall and began to paint.

It was fun! I painted the window so that it looked three-dimensional. The method is called *trompe l'oeil*.

Remember, I did go to art school.

I was painting an Italian scene in a French style, in Texas. I'm so worldly!

I spent days on this mural. It felt great to express myself with paint and color. I didn't realize it then but I'd desperately needed to do it. I'd spent so much energy taking care of Kelley through all of the medicines and hospital stays, but this project was completely for me.

Of course the good feelings didn't last.

People would come over and be amazed at the mural.
"Wow! This is beautiful!"
"Did you paint this yourself?"

And right when I would be feeling good about my hard work and talent, my husband would cut in and say, "Well, she's not finished. See, she made a mistake right here."

Again, I felt completely knocked down, all my creative energy squashed.

But now, as I looked around my beautiful teal living room, I felt empowered. *Omg, I love this space!*

My mind snapped back to the present again, in my beautiful teal living room. I poured a glass of Cabernet and sat down. Try to find the mistake now!

Cheers!

I sipped the wine and took in the beautiful color. I felt like I'd just reclaimed a piece of me.

What are your Eye-Poppin' colors?

I didn't realize it at first, but that teal is one of my eye-poppin' colors. One day a girlfriend was visiting and as we stood by my freshly-painted wall she said, "Wow! That color perfectly matches your eyes. You should totally get a top in that color!"

She was awesomely right! When I wear that color, I carry with me the same energy I feel in that room. I feel amazing.

When you align the colors you're wearing with the natural colors of your eyes, you create this amazing balance of energy. You just feel it. You know those colors look good on you, and you will probably get the most compliments when you wear them.

Your eyes are not just one color. They're made up of a suite of colors. Mine, for example, are a combination of sky-blue, turquoise, seafoam green, and light yellow. Ok, so teal isn't actually a color in my eyes, but teal does bring out the green-blue combination. In fact, my eyes really pop when I wear turquoise. When I wear bright sky blue, my eyes look like a purer blue. It's like magic.

You may not have this much variation in your eyes and that's okay. Your goal is to find the colors that enhance the colors of *your* eyes.

Take a long look at your eyes. Notice the different shades and tints of color. Do you have any of these colors in your closet? Hold them up to your face.

Even the darkest eyes have color, but it might be hard to see. If your eyes are dark, take a photo of your eyes in natural outdoor light; this will bring out the color. Your dark brown eyes might have blue-brown or even a purplish tint. You might see red-brown or golden yellow.

Find tops and dresses in your eye-poppin' colors. Paint or decorate a room in these colors. Where else could you add these colors?

There is something enchanting about these eye-poppin' colors. The more you make your eyes stand out, the more captivating you become to other people. People can't help but say, "Wow! I never noticed how blue your eyes are!" Your eyes are the focal point of your face, so why wouldn't you want to enhance their beauty?

Sign into the online companion course to see lots of examples of your Eye-Poppin' Colors.

YourColorStyle.com/bookgift

Your Statement Color

❋ ❋ ❋

What's next? I wondered with newly inspired energy. As I sipped my cabernet, I noticed how the room felt like me. An expression of me.

A roaring fire was suddenly lit inside me and I was ready to add more color into my world. I wanted to walk into each room and feel good. What if every room could feel like a perfect expression of me?

I headed into my kitchen for a little more celebratory wine and glanced over at the eating area. A small, tired kitchen table stood in the middle of the large rectangular space, dwarfing it into dollhouse size. Three matching and equally scraped, worn chairs circled the table.

What happened to that fourth chair again?

I felt energy begin to drain from my body, just looking at this sad display. These were the table and chairs we had bought for our first apartment. It was time for a change. I wanted to add energy into this room. What color should I add there?

Red. I love red. I've always wanted red leather chairs around a dining table.

The idea and the sudden warmth returning to my chest made me smile. I pulled my laptop out from under a pile of paint samples and opened it. Typing in "Red Leather Dining Chairs," I launched into an evening of scouring different sites, reading reviews, and comparing descriptions. When I'd finally made my decision I almost felt my stomach tighten as I clicked the submit button to order six red leather dining chairs.

Exactly three business days later, I placed six red leather chairs around my kitchen table and literally felt the energy level rise in the room. Ok, if I'm being perfectly honest, only four chairs fit because the table was so small. The other two chairs were placed against the wall. Still, it was a good start.

I sat in my dining room, on one of my new red leather chairs, taking in the colors of my home and the new emotions that were bubbling. Warmth. Passion. Energy.

The more decisions I made about what I really wanted in my home, the more confidence I felt in myself.

I was loving the creative process and I wasn't even close to done. This was only the beginning. I still needed to get a new table!

What are your Statement Colors?

Your statement colors are the ones that you choose to influence the *meaning* and *mood* for an event or space in your life. You may, without even knowing why, gravitate to one specific color and identify it as your personal statement color. It's the color that always jumps out at you—the color that, if you could, you would put everywhere to inspire you. This isn't necessarily a color you would wear, although you can of course. It's more about using the power of the color to influence how you want a situation or space to feel.

You may want more than one statement color, or you may opt to change it up based on your life events and environment and what energy you need more of at any given time.

There are two methods you can use to identify your statement color. The first is to look around your world and notice the colors that repeatedly show up. Is this a color that inspires you and makes you feel strong? You may already intuitively know your statement color and may even be using it unconsciously.

If you don't have a clear idea of what your statement color is, that's okay too. If your statement color isn't coming to you naturally, then you can start by making a conscious choice based on what you need and begin bringing color into your world with purpose.

Start with the questions:
- "How do I want this space to feel?"
- "How do I want to be seen or perceived?"
- "How do I want to feel?"
- "What energy do I want to create at this event?"

Based on your answer, you can choose a color that aligns with your purpose. Do you want your living room to have a joyful and bright mood? Then perhaps you would pop yellow into your space through fabrics, accessories, or wall color. Maybe you are going to a joyful event and you want to match the mood by wearing a yellow dress. If the color yellow truly inspires you in a way you can't explain, then consider weaving yellow into other areas of your life. Maybe a vase of yellow flowers on your desk at work. How about a bright yellow car?

Below is a list of colors, along with the mood and energy they bring. Choose the color that has the energy you want to bring into your life. Then add that color to your environment. It may be clothes, accessories, decorations, or objects. Have fun and play with this!

Red
Passionate, Sexy, Energetic
As I mentioned earlier, I personally love red. Popping it into a space adds energy and passion. Wearing it will bring attention to you. Wearing *all* red, like a red dress and bright shoes, adds a sexy powerful vibe to your appearance.

Red-Orange
Spicy, Heat, Energy
Red-orange or tomato red is a mix of red and orange. It conveys the passion and energy of red with the fun and enthusiasm of orange. It is a color of spice and heat. Wearing it will convey a sense of adventure.

Orange

Enthusiasm, Exciting, Optimistic, Fun

Orange is a mix of red and yellow. It conveys the energy of red with the joyfulness of yellow. Wearing an orange dress, for example, sends the message that you are fun and exciting. A little bit of it goes a long way. An bowl of fresh oranges or a few orange pillows immediately add a fun vibe into a space.

Dark Orange to Brown

Earthiness, Dependability, Strength

Dark orange and brown are the color of earth. These are grounding colors. When you wear them, you appear solid and dependable. Adding brown to a room grounds the room and adds comfort and warmth.

Yellow

Fun, Joyful, Happy

Yellow is a happy color and will brighten up any space. Imagine a bowl of lemons or a splash of yellow fabric. Wearing it sends the message that you are a happy and outgoing person. You could be as bold as wearing a yellow dress or pants, or just sprinkle it on in fun ways, like a pair of bright yellow shoes.

Green

Healthy, Growth, Abundance, Nature

Green is a mixture of yellow and blue. It has equal parts cool and warm. Wearing green can project the feeling of growth and prosperity. It is a hopeful color and might be worn to inspire. Adding it to your space creates a healthy, positive vibe. Consider plants to bring nature inside. A painted green accent wall is perfect for any space in which you want to promote good health and mental growth.

Turquoise
Cool, Fresh, Soothing, Fluidity
Turquoise is a mix of blue and green and is the color of the Caribbean Sea. It soothes and refreshes. Turquoise also happens to be a flattering color on most people. Wearing it creates a healthy, fresh, and very relaxed vibe. Adding it to a room will give the room a calming energy.

All Blues
Intelligent
Blue is a universal color and can be worn by anyone. If you want to be taken seriously, wearing blue is your best color choice.

Sky Blue
Peaceful, Spiritual
Sky blue is that beautiful blue you see on a sunny day. It's a color that can be worn by anyone. As a lighter, less

intense blue, it has a peaceful vibe. Adding it to a room gives the space a calming quality.

Dark Blue

Power, Depth, Stability, Trust

The darker the color, the more serious your message. Wearing dark blue or navy will send the message that you have authority and power. This is one of the reasons you often see police officers and business leaders wearing it. When you need to be seen as someone in a leadership position, navy blue is an excellent choice. You can also combine it with another color to lighten the mood. By the way, dark blue is often a better choice than black, which comes across as formal.

Bright Blue

Energetic, Bold

Bright colors hold a lot of energy. Wearing a bright blue, as with any bright color, will attract attention. Wearing it communicates that you are bold and outgoing.

Light Blue

Delicate, Ethereal, Calm

The lighter the blue, the calmer the energy. You'll notice that hospital rooms and walls of professional spaces are often painted in light blues. It creates a calm and professional feel. Wearing it creates a calming feeling and also sends a calming energy. Try wearing light blue pajamas or get some light blue bath towels.

Purple
Regal, Authoritative, Powerful, Spiritual
Purple is an even combination of red and blue. It has the passionate energy of red and the stability of blue. It is also a polarizing color—you either love it or hate it. Because of this, you may not want to wear purple to an event where you are concerned with how people will perceive you. If they hate the color, they may form a negative opinion of you. Purple is traditionally seen as a regal or spiritual color depending on the culture. A little bit of this color goes a long way.

Light Pink
Gentle, Soothing, Sweet, Tender
The lighter a color, the softer the energy and message. Light pink sends a gentle and caring vibe. It's the perfect color for a nursery and for nurse's scrubs. Wearing it will send the message that you are compassionate and gentle.

Pink
Open, Approachable, Friendly, Feminine
Pink is red with white added. The intensity of the red is softened and allows you to appear more approachable. Wear pink when you are with friends. Combining pink with navy blue will add a feminine quality to a serious

color. The more pink you wear, the more feminine and light-spirited you will appear.

Bright Pink
Whimsical, Fun, Exotic
Not everyone can wear bright pink. It is a bold color and looks best on someone that wants to be the center of attention. Wearing bright pink says that you are ready for fun. Splashing some into a room expresses whimsy.

Black
Mysterious, Formal, Dark, Strength, Sophisticated
Combining or adding black to a color will darken the mood of that color. Wearing a black dress or suit says that you are serious and formal. Wearing all black can also give a sophisticated and stylish vibe.

Grey
Strength, Solidity, Quiet, Sedate, Wisdom
Grey is black with white added. It is a color expressing wisdom and strength. Wearing grey will communicate the message of quiet, strong, and solid. It is best worn in high-quality fabrics like suits, shimmery gowns, and sweaters. Bringing grey into a room creates a quiet and sedate space, plus it is an excellent backdrop for popping in some bright color.

White and Cream
Honest, Good, Pure, Holy

It's no mystery why weddings often use white and cream in their decor. The mood is traditionally about purity, holiness, and truth. Many brides will opt for the purity of white in their dress but balance that with colorful bridesmaids' dresses and flowers to add personality to the event. Wearing an all-white suit or white sweater and pants will convey honesty. An all-white room, like a bathroom with plush white towels, communicates a sense of purity and cleanliness. It is a perfect backdrop to allow another color to be center stage. Combining or adding it to a color will lighten the mood of that color.

Time to Make a Statement
Surrounding yourself with your statement color will give you the strength you need to take on any life situation. Here are some creative ways to weave your statement color into your life:

- A pen and/or its ink color
- Phone case
- Wallet
- Your shoes
- A bag
- Scarf
- Nail polish
- Bathing suit
- Jewelry
- Lipstick
- Wall art
- Vase
- Flowers or plants
- Furniture
- Lamp
- Pillows

Jen Thoden

- Window treatments
- Bedding
- Rug
- Bowl of objects
- Glassware or dishes
- Placemats
- Cookware
- Car
- Wall color
- Towels
- Bath soap

Your Blushing Colors

❊ ❊ ❊

I stood in front of my bathroom mirror wearing a blouse that I'd recently bought. It was coral pink with a subtle shimmer. I knew that a color that matches the blush in your cheeks is one of the most flattering colors you can wear, but when I put it on, I began to doubt myself.

Does this color even look right on me? People are definitely going to notice this—what will they say? Is it too much?

In college, I dated a guy who turned out to have quite a controlling personality. He was a great-looking guy and I admit that I was completely swept away with the idea that that he wanted to date me. I didn't have a whole lot of confidence in myself and didn't like the way I looked, so when he asked me out, it was a huge boost to my ego.

We had fun in the beginning, but our dates became more and more stressful. First, he began to dictate how I wore my hair. Then it was how I dressed. There were evenings when he wouldn't leave the apartment until I put on exactly what he wanted me to wear, even if I didn't feel comfortable wearing it. Getting dressed became all about how he felt and he didn't seem to care about my feelings at all.

It's no surprise that I began to think of dressing up or looking attractive as a negative thing. I just wanted to hide in my baggy sweats and become invisible.

Yes, that relationship was poison and I soon broke it off, but it was an ugly time in my life and I carried those feelings with me for quite a while.

So you can imagine that the idea of wearing a strong color actually was quite terrifying for me.

And then there was what happened with my ex.

About two years before my divorce, I was sick of how I looked and felt. I'd put on nearly 30 pounds after Kelley's death, and I decided to do something about it. So I started to take care of myself. I watched what I was eating and I started running again.

I'd started a new job, and being back in an office setting and wanting to wear nice clothes again was a big motivator for this transformation. Eventually, I lost the weight, began to feel better about myself, and bought new clothes. I was enjoying my results!

Until my husband accused me of having an affair.

No, I wasn't having an affair. I was simply trying to look and feel good. I realize now that this new, improved version of me made him feel insecure.

Once again, feeling good and looking good came with a price. All the joy had drained out of me again.

"Get over it, Jen." I spoke softly to the woman in the mirror and turned sideways to examine my profile.

I wish I didn't care so much what other people think, but I am not going to change this top. I just finished my hair!

I stood up straighter with my hands on my hips and looked into the mirror again.

Hmm. I actually look pretty good! The coral pink really does pick up the color in my cheeks.

That day, I fell in love with this color and its effect on me and everyone around me.

It's actually soft and quiet. Pretty. Feminine. And that's how I felt. Pretty and feminine. And you know what? I received so many compliments at work that day!

"Did you lose weight?"
"Wow, you look great today!"
"Did you get your hair highlighted?"
"That color looks so pretty on you!"

By late morning, I was positively beaming! It was exactly what I needed. My confidence soared. My energy level picked up as the day went on. It was amazing how just a splash of color could make such a huge difference in how people saw me and how I saw myself.

What are your Blushing Colors?

I got all of those compliments that day because coral pink is my blushing color. I feel amazing in it, and I wear it whenever I want to feel pretty and feminine.

Your blushing colors are the colors that show on your cheeks when you blush or feel flushed. When you wear one of these, you may not even need to wear makeup. The color itself adds a healthy, youthful glow to your appearance. Who doesn't love that?

To find your blushing colors, go for a brisk walk or climb some stairs to get the blood into your cheeks and then look in the mirror. That's the color you want to wear.

Depending on the color of your skin, you might see red-orange, pastel pink, coral pink, plum, or salmon. From now on, when you see a top or dress in this color, get it!

You can also bring this color into your bedroom as a wall color, bedding, candles, or pajamas. When you begin and end the day in your blushing colors, it brings a cozy positive energy that can enhance your world.

Your blushing colors are like a secret power. Most people think of red or blue as the only colors that get attention, but wearing colors that enhance your natural blush will earn you second glances and endless compliments.

Do yourself a favor and accept these compliments graciously.

Don't deflect them or say something like, "Oh, but I'm feeling so tired today," or, "Thanks, it's really nothing," or whatever it is you say to yourself when you think you don't deserve something. Modesty is actually your bitchy ego trying to keep you feeling like your old self.

Stay aware and if positive energy is coming your way, soak it up, lady! You deserve to look and feel amazing every day. You got this!

Sign into the online companion course to see lots of examples of your Blushing Colors.

YourColorStyle.com/bookgift

Your Happy Color

❊❊❊

"My point!" I exclaimed after blasting the ping-pong ball just past his paddle. I playfully glared at my thirteen-year-old son, Matthew, as I picked up another ball. With a competitive stare, he stood in anticipation at the other end of our new ping-pong table. He swept his wavy hair from his sweaty forehead and smiled back. We were playing so hard that we'd managed to heat up the garage in December.

I'm kicking his butt!

I served another little white ball cleanly just over the net and Matt returned it with a powerful smack. I reached back to try to connect, but my paddle hit the wall behind me. The ping-pong table fit pretty nicely in the garage, but there wasn't much room for heroic moves.

"Got you, Mom!" Matt burst out between giggles.

This is such a great time!

I'd always loved ping-pong, but I'd never thought that having a ping-pong table could be so much fun. Well, not until I had bought it a couple weeks after that "Life By Design" coaching call.

The day after that call, I'd returned from the grocery store and parked my car in the driveway behind my garage. As the door squeaked and rattled open, I cringed at the disaster inside before loading up my arms with grocery bags, shutting the car trunk with my elbow and the door with my hip, and walking through the garage towards the house.

What a mess.

The previous owners of my townhouse had done a really nice job with the garage. They'd installed wall-to-wall commercial carpeting and finished all the walls. It was pretty nice for a garage, except that it was packed with the leftovers of my previous life. Unopened boxes, bolts of fabric (never used), and piles of assorted clutter against the walls made for a serious mess. I couldn't even park my car in there.

As I navigated the one narrow path through the stacked boxes, I could hear the voice of my life coach, "How can you add creativity and fun to this space?" I stopped and took a long look around.

If I cleaned out this space, I could turn it into a rec room. Sure, I could make room for my car, but where's the fun in that?

My eyes stopped at the pile of soccer balls, the deflated basketball, other miscellaneous outdoor gear, and...

Tennis rackets? Oooh! Table tennis... Yes! A ping-pong table! This is the perfect place for one.

My self-confidence had been growing steadily since I had begun infusing color into my home and wardrobe, but I couldn't honestly say that I'd been having more fun. At least not with the kids.

When was the last time I had fun with the kids?

After putting the groceries away, I called the junk guys to pick up all the fabric and donatables. A lot of the rest of it went into the trash. Such a relief to have it gone!

I painted the garage walls a fun blue. And I bought the ping-pong table.

Unique, super-organized Matt helped put it together and a few hours later we played. It was a blast. We played every weekend after that, and it was some of the best fun I'd ever had with my kids up to then.

After that particularly intense game of ping-pong, I sat on the couch, watching Matt practice tricks with a deck of playing cards.

Why haven't I allowed myself to have so much crazy fun with my kids? What held me back?

Immediately, my thoughts flashed back to an evening I'd spent with all three kids—Kelley, Matt, and Mindy—watching *The Polar Express*. They were probably eight, six, and four years old, and they were mesmerized by the movie. It was just before Christmas and this movie put us into the holiday spirit. It was such a "normal" moment, which was highly unusual for us.

"Normal" for us was spending uncomfortable nights in the hospital while Kelley suffered through pain and nausea from chemotherapy. "Normal" was knowing she would likely not make it to Christmas.

I remember trying not to think about that prognosis as we all watched the movie. The doctors clearly had to be wrong, because there she was, cuddled up next to me.

Hold onto this moment, I told myself.

Two months later, Kelley lost her battle with cancer, at only nine years old. I had lost my little girl, and Matt and Mindy had lost their big sister. We now had a space in our lives that would take a long time to fill.

I don't know if losing Kelley is the only reason I don't feel like I'd enjoyed my kids, I thought as I watched Matt concentrate on his trick. Looking back, I could see many times when it was easier to focus on the day-to-day tasks and not engage with them.

"Hey Mom, watch this," Matt said as he fanned the cards out in one hand.

"Nice!" I cheered and tousled his hair before getting up to drink some water (ping-pong makes me thirsty!) and soak the dishes.

Jen Thoden

I was in a grey cloud for a long time, but I feel like I'm finally waking up. The color is flowing back into my life and I see what I've been missing out on. And I finally know that I can do whatever I want. I don't need permission to think, feel, do, or not do, anything, Wow!

I looked up at my kitchen and the sexy red chairs at my dining room table and smiled.

Do what I want? Why does this feel like such a new concept at forty years old?

As I turned on the water and began rinsing the dishes, I reflected on all of the things I had done to make other people happy.

Ugh… camping!

I shook my head as I continued to rinse dishes and remembered one of the first moments I'd decided to honor my own desires.

For years, my husband insisted we go on camping trips, despite the fact that I didn't like it. In fact, it's more accurate to say that I absolutely hated it. We'd pack up the kids, the camping gear, the dog, the food, the bug spray and sunscreen, and whatever else we needed to survive a night or two outside and load it all into the Jeep. I'd done it enough times to know for sure that it wasn't my thing. I actually enjoyed hiking—that feeling of exploring a trail and discovering a waterfall or creek along the way was always fun for me. But once we finished the hike, I just wanted to go home and take a hot shower, not lie on cold rocky ground, stuffed into a sleeping bag with dried up sweat and dirt. By morning, my neck and back would ache and I'd start the day already feeling exhausted.

And then of course, if I needed to use the restroom in the middle of the night, I'd have to find my way to the smelly public facilities in complete darkness, armed only with a flashlight, hoping to not get eaten by a bear or some other hungry animal. Not my thing. No thanks. I didn't feel one with nature and didn't care to. And no, squatting in the woods was absolutely not an option!

Near the end of our marriage, my husband recruited our friends for our camping weekends. Since I was no longer in the mood to do something just to keep the peace, I said, "No thanks." It took him a while to process this, as if it had never occurred to him that I had a choice.

What's ironic is that it had never occurred to *me* that I had a choice. But there is almost always a choice. That day, I chose not to camp one more day of my life. I'll hike. I'll happily sleep in a bed in a cute cabin. I won't sleep in a zipped bag on a cold slab of rock with bugs crawling on me. I don't care if the snakes will eat the bugs. And I don't even want to think about what will eat the snakes.

So he opted to go without me, and it was nice to enjoy a night alone to watch movies and relax in a quiet house. I ignored the guilt I felt because I deserved those quiet moments.

Why was I always the one to compromise?

Dishes finally done, I washed the sink out and thought about how good it felt to design my own life.

Now I'm designing my life the way I want it to be. Adding color and fun into all aspects of it. Speaking of fun, it's time for another ping-pong game!

I turned off the sink and poked my head into the living room. "Round 2?"

Matt's head snapped up to flash a huge smile before he leapt off the couch and ran down to the garage, where we happily continued to dive, laugh, and zing balls back and forth for two more hours.

What are your Happy Colors?

Your Happy Colors are the brighter colors that you just love but maybe never wear. The whole point to the story I just shared with you is to think about those things that truly bring you joy and give yourself permission to enjoy them. You need to give yourself permission to wear your happy colors too!

I can't tell you how many times I've stared at a bright pink top, secretly loving it and wishing I could wear it. And then do nothing. Sometimes I'd actually buy the top and hang it proudly in my closet, only to convince myself daily that it was not the right time to wear that bright color. I'd move right past that happy option and choose something less special.

I'd tell myself that it was silly to wear pink or that I should only wear that color for special occasions. I'd worry that I wouldn't look good in it or that I would somehow be the subject of mean conversations.

Here's a big tip: People don't care about what you wear nearly as much as you think they do. Unless of course you're Wonder Woman; then people seem to care a lot! But generally, they've got their own things to deal with. It's taken me a long time to build up the confidence to wear that bright pink without worrying if somebody else would like it.

Bright watermelon pink is now one of my go-to colors. It brightens me up. I feel confident in it. I like the way I look when I wear this color, and I like giving myself permission to wear something that makes me happy.

Think about a bright color that makes you smile. A color that brings you joy just by looking at it. Maybe it's a color that's a little scary to wear. It could be a pattern. Maybe you love red and white stripes or yellow polka dots. Or maybe it's the combination of blue and green together. It doesn't matter what the color is, as long as it brings you that sensation of joy.

If wearing your happy color isn't your thing yet, then try a fashion scarf in that color. They're inexpensive and easy to wear and experiment with. Still not sure? Then pop your happy color into your home. Hang art that has that color. Get a chair or pillow in that color.

That said, I encourage you to stretch yourself and try wearing your happy color. Each time you do, your self-confidence will grow. You may even begin to trust your judgment and see that you truly can do anything you want. You are the designer of your life.

Sign into the online companion course to watch a video about your Happy Colors.

<u>YourColorStyle.com/bookgift</u>

Jen Thoden

Your Grounding Colors

❋ ❋ ❋

The evening air was crisp as Joe and I walked home from the grocery store. We were in good moods and chatting about our upcoming Thanksgiving trip to the beach with his family. The plan was to rent a big house in Florida with his parents, his three siblings, their spouses, and all the kids.

Joe looked forward to this trip every year and was excited to share a new idea with me: "Why don't we *drive* down to the beach this year instead of flying?" He glanced at me over the full grocery bag he carried.

"Umm, no way," I said dismissively, looking down at the ground. "You are not putting me in a car for two long-ass days each way!"

"Why not? It'll be fun. We can stop at The Varsity for chili-cheese dogs and onion rings! We'll fill the car with snacks. Plus, it'll save us a lot of money."

Joe loves himself a road trip. Two days in the car is nothing to him. He has lists of places to stop and things to eat along the way. It's relaxing and enjoyable to him.

But me? My cheeks heated and tears welled up in my eyes as I responded, "If you want to drive, I'd rather not go."

Joe stopped and turned toward me. He clearly hadn't expected this reaction and seemed annoyed, which didn't help the tears one bit.

If only he understood how miserable a long car ride is to me!

I get incredibly motion-sick. I can't read in the car. Stop-and-go traffic triggers my nausea. Riding the train to work is my own personal hell. Once, while traveling from DC to New York on the Acela Express train, I had to run to the bathroom to violently throw up. I must have looked awful because the cashier at the snack bar just handed me a bottle of sparkling water without a word.

To make things worse, I have suffered through endless road trips, pretty much held hostage in the car. Every summer, my ex-husband, the kids, and I would drive to North Carolina for our beach trip. The drive was anywhere from six to eight hours, depending on traffic. And there was *always* traffic. Slow down. Stop. Speed up. Slow down. STOP! I just wanted to shoot myself.

It's guaranteed that I'm going to feel nauseous riding in the car. If I don't have anything to drink to settle my stomach, I will have to throw up. I'm a treat, I know, but it's not my fault. In fact, I'm fine if I can just drive for a bit. Except of course, my ex would never let me. So I'd lean my head against the window and quietly deal with it, fighting the urge to insist we pull over. He'd just sigh as if I were being overly dramatic.

If that wasn't enough, at some point I'd need to use the restroom. Before we had kids, he simply wouldn't pull over until it made sense for *him* to stop. I'd be in crazy pain to the point that when I finally got to a restroom, my bladder would be in such a state of shock that it would take like twenty minutes to go, which just made things worse with him. I was so relieved—literally!—when we had kids. Small bladders always win! When they have to go, it's already too late. So we would pull over pretty often for them, which was a big plus for me.

Joe isn't like him, I tried to convince myself as I stood in front of a man who had proven his empathy and understanding on many occasions. *But it's still a twenty-hour road trip!*

"I'll fly and meet you down there," was all I could muster through my tears before I started walking again.

We walked the rest of the way home in silence.

"It won't be the same as driving with him, Jen," he said after setting the groceries on the counter. "We'll take our time. We'll stop whenever you want. You can drive as much as you want. Or you can just take motion-sickness medicine and sleep the whole way."

I took a deep breath and looked up into his eyes. "Ok," I whispered.

Maybe he's right. Maybe I'll enjoy the trip. There are still so many things I'm learning about myself.

When the day arrived and the car was packed, I selected my road-trip outfit. Of course there was a road trip outfit!

It was freezing in Virginia so I chose a golden camel sweater poncho with black leggings and black boots.

We stopped for breakfast on our way out of town and I looked up to see Joe smiling at me across the table. "You look very pretty."

I loved the compliment. I really felt good in these colors. They had a warm, golden quality that felt calming and grounded to me, which was exactly what I would need for twenty hours on the road.

Turns out, the road trip was actually fun. I drove for a while, and then took a non-drowsy motion-sickness medicine that immediately knocked me unconscious. So much for non-drowsy. Let's just say that I arrived at our first stop *very* rested.

Joe made it super easy to travel without anxiety. I felt completely at home with him. In fact, I enjoyed the trip so much that we've since taken a second road trip to Walt Disney World in a rented minivan with Mindy and Jack. I can't believe I'm even writing this, but I've learned that I actually like road trips! I still want to stop quite often, but it's great to enjoy the journey and not be rushed to the destination. There's a life lesson in there somewhere, but maybe that's another book.

What are your Grounding Colors?

That feeling of being calm and grounded is exactly what your grounding colors will do for you. It's like getting to know yourself all over again.

For me, golden browns, creams, and camels are my go-to grounding colors. I can find these colors in my hair and eyebrows. I typically wear these colors in the fall and winter. In the spring and summer, I prefer navy blue that works with the dark grey blue around my iris. These colors enhance my natural coloring and tone.

Your grounding colors are basically your neutrals, but they're more than JUST neutrals. They should reflect the essence of you. These colors will be a combination of personal preference and your natural coloring. They may also change from season to season, as darker colors may only work for you personally in the cold months.

To find your grounding colors, take a look at your natural hair color and your eyebrows. If you can't decide, look in your eyes. Do you have a dark ring around your iris? The colors you see may help you decide.

If you have soft, cool tones, your grounding colors may be grey, grey-blue, or white. If you have dark hair, fair skin and blue eyes, your grounding colors may be black, white, or pewter grey.

Your grounding colors are like a security blanket, in that it feels easy to wear them. You can wear them on their own or combine them with your other colors. Ideally they should work well with your other signature colors, but they don't have to.

What's most important is that you find a set of go-to neutrals that you really like wearing and that help you feel grounded and secure in your own skin.

Sign into the online companion course to see lots of examples of your Grounding Colors.

YourColorStyle.com/bookgift

Pulling It All Together

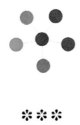

✻ ✻ ✻

Blending families is not easy. It's not like The Brady Bunch, where everyone moves into the same house and mostly lives happily ever after. It's challenging, and in our case, our combined family is sometimes more like a bubbly emulsion of oil and water than a smooth blend.

First, our kids could not be more different. Second, unlike Joe and me, they didn't *choose* to be together.

He and I have different personalities and parenting styles, so it's not surprising that we have very different children. My two, Matt and Mindy, are competitive. They like to play sports and it's super important to win. They're both very independent and not too long ago, my main role in their lives seemed to be driving them from soccer game to soccer game. They also seem to share one brain!

Often, when one begins a thought, the other finishes it. They're incredibly close, but they weren't always that way.

In fact, for a long time, Mindy was the outsider and Kelley and Matt were a unit. Mindy drove Matt nuts. She would follow him and stay on his heels, annoying him to the point of madness. I can't tell you the number of times I heard, "Stop it! Stop following me! Stoooppp!" Then, WHACK! And screams of pain that honestly could be coming from any of them. But when Kelley got sick, Matt was left on his own and soon found an eager companion in Mindy. They have been inseparable ever since.

Joe's son Jack is completely opposite. He isn't into sports, but he loves video games and photography. He truly has an artist's eye. He's okay sometimes with not winning, and instead relishes the experience of everybody playing together. The biggest differentiator for Jack, though, is that he's an only child. He's had the loving attention of both his parents all his life with zero competition from other siblings.

You can imagine Jack's reaction when Matt and Mindy rolled into his life with noise, laughter, competitiveness, rough-and-tumble activities, and countless private jokes. Mindy and Matt fill a room simply by being in it and Jack seemed to feel pushed out. Those early days were tough on all of us, but maybe mostly on Jack.

We tried not to force the kids together, as that seemed painful and unnecessary, but we still needed to figure out how to operate together as a family.

Fortunately for all of us, Joe became the central pillar in our blended family and pulled us all together. Matt and Mindy adore him. Jack prefers his dad to me, of course. And well… *I* married him!

Joe's the center of our wheel with four spokes circling him.

Your five Signature Colors are like a blended family. Some colors go well together. Some don't seem to mesh at all. You might have some loud colors and some quieter ones. You might have one or two that regularly hang out together in multiple outfits, and others that prefer going solo.

So how do you avoid having a closet of colors and still nothing to wear?

Well, you need one color that's the central pillar to your other colors, like Joe is the center in our family even when we don't always harmonize with one another. This core color plays the key role in creating outfits with your other colors, and this is where it gets exciting! You can always choose a neutral or your grounding color as a core color, and it will likely go with all of your other colors. That's the easiest way to start.

Or you can be a bit more adventurous. What if your core color is, well, another color? Crazy, right? It's a color that will act like a neutral but may not be your typical beige, grey, or black. This may be a color that you could change out depending on the season in order to breathe new life into your wardrobe.

And remember, even if your signature colors don't all go together, you should absolutely try to have all five colors in your closet and somewhere in your space.

If you do this, it becomes a beautiful, authentic reflection of *you*.

Time To Pull It All Together

This exercise will help you chart your signature colors and show you how you can eventually add even more to your wardrobes and spaces.

First, you'll need a color wheel. You can find a color wheel in your free gifts at YourColorStyle.com/bookgift

Now, it's time to plot out your five signature colors on the color wheel the way I did in **Figure 2.0 below.** If one of your colors is actually a neutral, then you can skip that one.

Next, create triangles starting with two of your colors. This isn't an exact science, but it's a fun way to get an idea of another color that might work with your signature colors. The idea here is to draw a line connecting two of your signature colors, then figure out a third point on the wheel that will form an equilateral triangle (or close to it) with the two points you just picked. The triangles should be close to an equilateral triangle—one in which all three sides are the same length.

As you can see in Figure 2.0, I was able to create three triangles with my colors. They all point to an area of the color wheel that has olive greens and golden browns. Oh yeah! I like the idea of adding olive green as a core color.

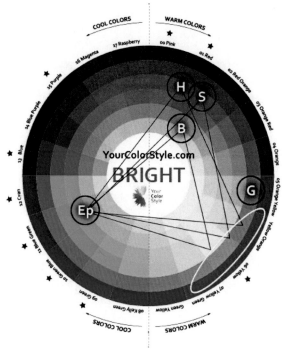

Figure 2.0

EP = Eye-Poppin' Colors
B = Blushing Colors
H = Happy Colors
S = Statement Colors
G = Grounding Colors

My signature color palette looks something like this:

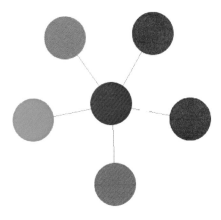

Your signature colors are your go-to colors. You can always count on looking amazing in these colors. Plus, knowing your signature colors will make shopping easy and outfit-styling fun.

Taking Back Your Power

❉ ❉ ❉

I can't believe I'm doing this, I thought as I stood among a crowd of people anxiously waiting for the race to start. A half marathon. Over thirteen miles.

I'd never done anything like this before. Sure, I'd run a 5K race before but this was so much longer. I looked around at the runners next to me. Men and women of all ages with their race numbers pinned to their shirts.

They look like they know what they're doing... Do I? Maybe I should stretch or something.

I admit, I was pretty intimidated. There were over 2,000 people running this race and it looked like at least half of them were jammed up near the front of the queue.

"RUNNERS, LINE UP. FIVE MINUTES BEFORE WE START," the announcer's voice boomed over the speakers.

Ok, I got this.

Two-plus hours is a long time, but I felt good. I'd been training for this race for six months.

A cool morning spring breeze chilled my neck and I started bouncing on my feet to warm up. Honestly, I just wanted to look like I'd done this before.

This is what you do, right? Bounce on your feet to warm up?

And then, we were running.

More like a slow jog/walk/shuffle because there were so many people packed together trying to get over the start line.

It seemed to take forever but eventually I passed under the big, colorful arch that marked the start and finish line and I fell into an easy pace.

Jen Thoden

I'm really doing this!

Feeling more empowered with each decision I'd made for my life, I'd realized I needed to do something more *just for me.* Sure, I was adding color throughout my environments and wardrobe, and designing my life with my core values in mind. But I still felt like I needed to do something truly personal for me. A goal or milestone uniquely mine.

I wanted it to be something that felt almost impossible at the time, so that I could look back at it and say, "Yeah, I did that. I kick ass!"

I wanted to be a kick-ass marathon-running woman. Yep! That's what I wanted to do. Run killer races. How badass!

Ok, so I very quickly decided that I didn't want to run twenty-six miles, but I was up for figuring out how to run thirteen. I could run three already, so it was only like, ten more. How hard could that be?

"MILE 3," the sign read as I ran by.

Wow, three miles is as far as I used to run when I started training for this. Now three miles down already? What happened to the first two miles? Maybe this'll be easier than I thought!

The path was a winding, rutted dirt road through the hills of Virginia wine country. On either side of the road were countless small vineyards and rustic houses. Trees lined the road, offering cool shade.

I'm so glad I did this!

I felt a rush of happiness. My endorphins had kicked in and I was feeling good. I congratulated myself for overcoming some serious mind blocks just to be ready for this race. I had to truly reinvent myself as a *runner*, not just somebody who likes to run.

Go, me!

As I ran past the four-mile marker, I started a personal-development audiobook I'd loaded just for this race.

"Are you willing to do whatever it takes for the chance to live entirely on your own terms?" I heard the voice ask.

Heck yeah!

When I was initially looking at running long periods of time and distance, self-doubt and frustration had rushed in. How did people do this without keeling over from boredom?

As if to answer, I'd heard my life coach's voice ring through my mind, "How can you align your core values to your running?" (I constantly hear him in my head now—should I be worried?)

I went to work to include my core values into my running.

To Have Fun: I had my music playlist. Super fun! It is loaded up with music from shows like *Mamma Mia, Greece, Frozen,* and *Trolls.* Just listen to "Go the Distance," from the movie *Hercules.* It's so inspirational! I'd started building this playlist despite a touch of embarrassment about what people might think if they heard it. Honestly, I have no idea why I cared so much. Eventually I decided, *Who cares? If they hear a song and think it's silly, that's their problem.*

To Learn: Well, I was already learning something new. I'd never run more than three miles, so training to run more than thirteen was definitely keeping me energized to stay on track. But learning wasn't going to pull me through hours of running. Could it? What if I could learn something new *while* running? Thinking about how much I loved personal development books, and my new obsession with self-improvement since starting the life-coaching program, I decided to listen to audiobooks. It wouldn't hurt to try it, right?

For my first hour-plus run while training, I'd played the audiobook *Eat That Frog* by Brian Tracy and was stunned when the hour flew by! Plus, I was armed with mad skills to get stuff done. Soon, I began to look forward to those extremely long Saturday morning runs. Me, my route, my showtunes, my audiobooks, and my thoughts. It became my version of meditation.

And today, it's paying off big-time! I'm going to finish thirteen miles!

I watched the road in front of me very carefully. The dirt was packed fairly smooth but there were ruts and rocks that could easily twist an ankle. I glanced to my right as a runner passed me and noticed that she was wearing a bright turquoise top and running tights with a bright pink, blue, and turquoise swirl pattern.

How fun! That looks like one of my long-run outfits. Super-cute, even if she IS passing me.

(Hey, I'm competitive. What can I say?)

My running gear is super fun and colorful, but it didn't start out that way.

I'd always worn the typical black tights and tank top. Every time I dressed to run in those days, I felt like I was moving through mud. My running needed some creative inspiration! I was designing my life, right? Correction: I was designing ME. And I'm a badass running woman, so I need to run in full color! I bought myself bright tops, fun sports-bras, and silly-patterned leggings. That way, when I opened my drawer with all my fun colorful gear, I smiled. The colors gave me energy and inspiration to get moving and keep moving.

A little bit of cool rain hit my shoulders as we ran down a hill and around a bend.

"Good job!"
"Keep it up!"
"Way to go!"

A crowd cheered at the bottom of the hill and made me smile. My thighs were starting to burn and the hills were brutal, but I was inspired to push through.

Thanks, loud, encouraging people!

I was feeling really good.

Wait, what mile am I on?

I'd lost track a while back. I was only half-listening to my audiobook because my mind kept wandering. (Hey, whatever gets me through…)

Then I saw a large red barn with tables set out in front of it. Runners were jogging through, grabbing water, and using the potties.

Halfway! I've made it halfway!

I looked at my watch and realized I'd been running for more than an hour.

Yikes, that's why I gotta pee!

After taking care of business, I started jogging again, following the line of runners through the crowd. I laughed as I noticed people handing out little cups of wine to the runners and remembered this was a winery. Hilarious!

"No thanks," I waved as a volunteer offered me a taste of wine. I was already feeling tired and wine wasn't exactly going to help. (Maybe later though!) Instead, I grabbed an energy drink and an energy gel to help power me through the second half.

As I left the winery, the route backtracked down the road I'd just run. Runners were still coming down the opposite direction and I watched with glee as complete strangers slapped high-fives as they ran by.

"Way to go!" I cheered and clapped a fellow runner with a high-five.

"MILE 10" the marker read.

I'd been running for about an hour and forty-five minutes, and fatigue was now catching up to me. My upper-back was cramping up, my sides were stiff, my feet were sore, and I felt like my body was slowly imploding.

So close, but still another thirty minutes to go.

I looked around and saw people jogging and then walking.

Ok, this isn't feeling fun anymore. I gotta do something else or I'll end up walking. Then, I may never get moving again! I remembered the iPhone strapped to my arm. *Showtunes! Time to switch it up and get lost in some music that makes me smile.*

I carefully pulled my iPhone out of its armband. My sweaty hands made it tricky to keep from dropping it. Even more tricky was unlocking it as I focused on avoiding big rocks and holes on the unpaved road. I tapped my playlist.

"Let It Go" from the movie *Frozen* started playing.

"Let it go... let it goooo... can't hold it back anymore...."

I won't hold back anymore, Elsa. The cold never bothered me anyway.

I grinned ear to ear. Only three miles left. I remembered again that three miles was all I could do when I started training.

I can do this!

"MILE 12," said the marker. One mile left!

"Let's finish this!" I said out loud and started running with every last bit of energy I could muster. My body fell into a fluid pace as I ran through the burning sensation in my thighs and the pinch that had flared up in my right knee. I ran through the pain, the self-doubt, and the low self-esteem that my bitchy ego threw at me during the last mile. I ran through all of it.

I turned the corner and there was the finish line. My heart started pounding, in a good way.

This is it! Go! Ignore the pain and fatigue. Finish strong! Don't trip!

The thought of taking a tumble within sight of the finish line almost made me laugh.

I picked up my pace a little more. My body felt numb. My legs felt like jelly. My feet felt heavy.

And then, just like that, I was past the finish line. I heard my name over the speakers as I crossed the line in two hours and fifteen minutes. Jogging my way to a walk, I looked around.

I really did it! I just ran over two hours! If I can run thirteen miles, I can do anything.

I walked slowly to the snack table where I picked up a banana and some water and stayed to watch the other runners finish their races.

This was the first time that I had truly completed a goal that I'd set just for me. Like many people, I have a tendency to set goals but then either forget about them or convince myself that they weren't really goals I wanted to achieve.

It's so easy to not do something, I almost quit several times.

Early on in my training, I had to run five miles, which at the time was the farthest I had ever run. At mile four, my right knee started hurting and I ended up limping the last mile. During that long, painful walk back home, I'd almost convinced myself that this wasn't for me. Maybe I was too old to start training for that half marathon. What if I couldn't run more than forty-five minutes without injury? What if I got to the race and still couldn't run a full thirteen miles?

I knew I couldn't quit. I had to hold onto my definition of who I wanted to be. A runner. A badass woman who runs half-marathons. Badasses don't quit. They push through to goals that matter to them and wear their injuries like a badge of honor.

Running that race proved to me that I could do anything I wanted badly enough. It was one of the best things I'd ever done for myself.

YOU Matter

You don't have to run a half marathon to prove to yourself that you are important, but take the time to invest in your own life. To take care of YOU.

By the way, this isn't about being greedy or selfish; it's about being you.

I spent years living life for everybody else, giving myself completely to my kids and my husband. I don't think back on those times as being very happy. It was my job to be a good mom and wife; and at the time, I believed that meant that I should put my own needs last. Sure if there was an opening in the schedule, maybe I did something I wanted to do, but it almost never happened because I would simply guilt myself out of doing anything just for me.

I didn't realize it then, but every time I turned myself down and did something for someone else instead, I lost a little bit of myself. I was handing over my own power to whomever seemed to want it.

"Of course you should go golfing. I've got the kids, don't worry about it."

"You focus on work. I'll take Kelley to her doctor's appointment and then get Mindy from daycare and then stop to pick up Matt from kindergarten. No problem."

I didn't have to do all those things myself. I could have asked for help. I could have demanded a break or some time for myself, but I didn't.

That's on *me*.

It took losing a child and a marriage to wake me up to the fact that I matter.

And so do YOU.

This is your life, and it can be anything you want it to be. You don't need permission to live a happy and joyful life.

For me, adding color in small doses gave me confidence to do more for myself. Wanna hear the most ironic and best part? As I took back my own power and designed my own life, I became a much better mother and wife. I'm still working on me, and now I have an amazing husband and fantastic kids supporting me on my journey.

Who am I?

Writing this book was personally transformational. As much as I love art, I'd stopped drawing after Kelley's death and struggled to give myself the permission to get back into it. Ironically, even as I wrote about losing my artist self, I started illustrating for this book. At first, there were only a couple drawings but Joe encouraged me to add illustrations throughout the book. This wasn't the original plan but I absolutely loved doing it, and now this book has become a true reflection of my personality.

A truly unexpected result of producing this book, I now feel like I've come full circle.

I'm Jen Thoden. I am a mother, wife, author, vlogger, speaker, entrepreneur, color expert, runner, loud laugher, seeker of fun, lover of wine, beer, all things Disney, cruises, and… an artist.

Life is amazing. Get to know yourself and become who you want to be, one color at a time.

About Jen Thoden

Jen Thoden is a writer, speaker, entrepreneur, color expert, runner, and mother-of-the-year (not).

She is the international bestselling author of *That's My Color: Discover Your 5 Signature Colors and Transform Your Life.*

Her mission is to help women transform into happier versions of themselves by being true and authentic. She is the founder of <u>Your Color Style</u>™, a proprietary online color system that makes it easy for women to discover their best colors. Jen is the go-to expert on color, confidence, and authenticity. Her expertise has been featured in *Inc.com, She Knows,* and *Thrive Global.*

When she isn't hosting workshops, speaking, or writing, you can find her exploring a winery with Joe, relaxing on a cruise ship with her family, or loving life in Disney World. She lives in Ashburn, VA, with her husband, Joe, and three kids.

To contact Jen for speaking engagements or media interviews, please email <u>support@yourcolorstyle.com</u>

Connect with Jen

Website: JenThoden.com
Email: support@yourcolorstyle.com

Acknowledgments

❊ ❊ ❊

I cannot express enough gratitude for the following people in my life:

My husband, Joe: Thank you for being a true partner in life and my best friend. Thank you for your loving support throughout this journey. Thank you for your mad editing skills and for all those late night ideation sessions. This book is half yours in so many ways. I love you and I can't wait to write our next book together.

My parents: Thank you for telling me I can do whatever I want in life and believing in me. Thank you for your never-ending support and encouragement. I love you both.

My business and life coach, Phil: Thank you for being the voice that keeps me on track (even when I'm not actually talking to you!), for your masterful insight, and for the many laughs every Saturday morning. And thank you for encouraging me to share my story.

My book coach and editor, Amanda: Thank you for your amazing insight and making sense of my stories. You helped me convey my message in such a powerful way. You rock!

My amazing team (Sharon, Patricia, Mandy, and Matt): Thank you for running my business and providing amazing customer service. Thank you for helping me when I need it, before I need it, and even when I don't think I need it. You are amazing and I am so grateful for you.

Matthew, Mindy and Jack: Thank you for sharing your passions and interests with me. Thank you for being my fans and insisting on taking time to hang out with you. Thank you for your love, for your positive energy, and for believing in me. You inspire me in so many ways. I love you.

Jen Thoden

References

Gholipour, B. (2014, December 3). *Middle-Age Women Have Highest Rate of Depression.* Retrieved from https://www.livescience.com/48978-middle-age-women-highest-depression-rate.html